Down to Sea in Little Boats

Poems and Stories from the Life of a Fisherman

NORMAN LA VINE

Cover illustration: Alec La Vine Tritt
Book design: Lizzie Newell
Photos from the La Vine family

Distributed through Ingram

print ISBN: 978-1-942528-14-2
epub ISBN: 978-1-942528-15-9

For my sweetheart Angela. She gave me a life.

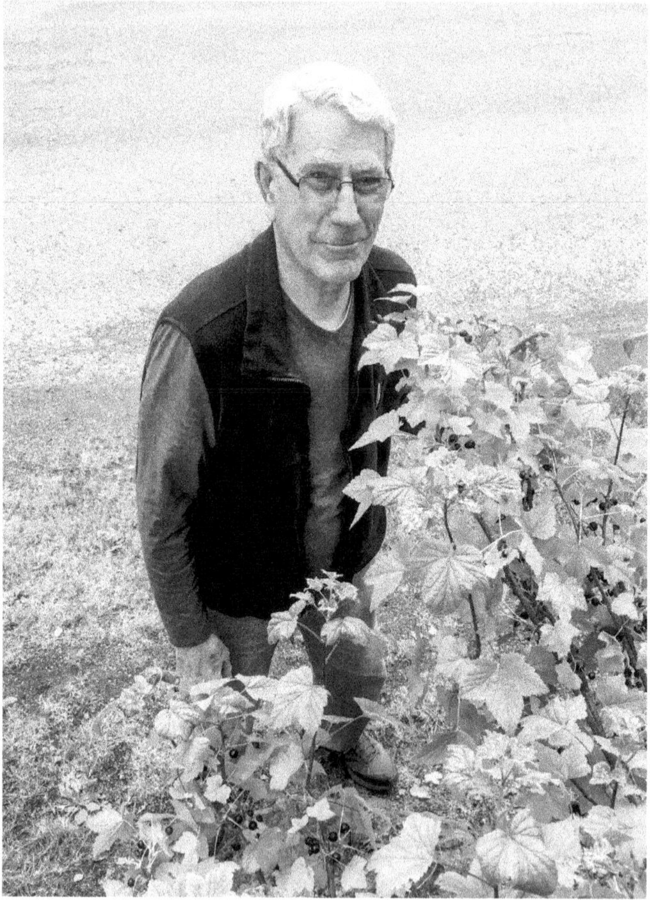

ABOUT THE AUTHOR

Norman La Vine is a former commercial fisherman, charter boat captain, and service vessel pilot who spent the majority of his life on the ocean. Norman got his first job as a deckhand in 1950 when he was fourteen years old. He bought his first boat, the *Thea Marie,* by the time he was twenty-one. Norman has traveled the waters off the West Coast of the United States from Baja California to the Midway Islands. Norman also worked as a vessel pilot in Louisiana, the Middle East, and Alaska.

After spending the majority of his life in California, Norman split his later years between Alaska and the beautiful Whidbey Island of Washington state with his lifelong love and wife, Angela. He now resides in Anchorage, Alaska with his daughter, son-in-law, two grandchildren, and their rough collie Hedge.

Robbin La Vine

CONTENTS

INTRODUCTION

Norman wrote his first story in high school and his last poem not long after his daughter was married in 2003. Most of his poems and stories were handwritten at sea in a growing number of small notebooks. Many of the stories and poems included in this book were never written down by Norman. Instead, these were stories told to family and friends so frequently that Robbin, his daughter, recalled them and they were finally written down after Norman returned to Alaska in his later years. Stories recorded in this way are: "Down to Sea in Little Boats," "Getting Acquainted with Dolphins," "A Full Hold and a Load on Deck," and "Tug Boat Irene." The story for which this book is named is the first story Norman remembers writing.

What is most significant to know about Norman and his craft as a storyteller, is that it wasn't until much later in life that he learned he had a disability. He was assessed to have dyslexia, a condition that led him to pick up a trade instead of continuing on to college.

Norman had a way with words in his younger years that began to fail him as he aged. Stories that he actually hand wrote over the course of his life display more artistry than those recited and finally written down by his daughter in later years, but they were treasured stories none-the-less. Robbin was careful not to embellish the stories beyond his simple telling.

Robbin recalls many evenings from her youth when, with friends over and dinner complete, Norman would pull out the notebooks and read stories to family and company. And if the guests happened to be writers as well, there would be a back and forth, a sharing of the post dinner stage.

In 2011, Norman's beloved wife and life partner, Angela, suffered a massive stroke from which she would never recover. Norman moved them both to Alaska to be closer to family. Angela passed away in July of 2012. After the move and the loss of his love, Norman began to review his stories and poems, some of which had been typed up by enthusiastic family and friends, but the vast majority remained in handwritten format. Over the course of six months, Norman typed all his handwritten stories and poems on his own. For someone who does not know how to type, this was quite a feat!

Robbin made initial edits for spelling and grammar but many more supportive people, friends and family, have contributed to the finalization of Norman's work in order to prepare for this publication. Norman would like to thank and acknowledge Kim Eden (his wife's niece), Dorothy Tomilson, Patricia Fay Morgan, Tre Lenehan, Lynne Curry, Lizzie Newell, and his daughter Robbin La Vine.

Robbin La Vine

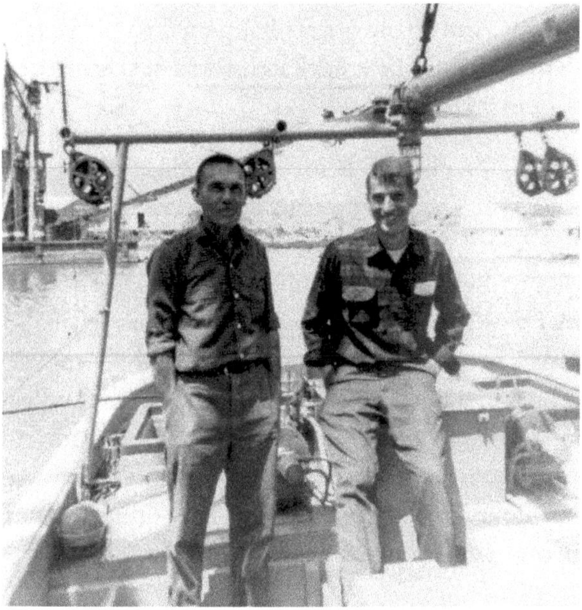

1964 Norman and Hank, captain of the *Nile II*.

BLESSED REDEEMER

Early 1970s

*T*he woman sat heavily at the kitchen table. Having put the children to bed and finishing the last of her chores, this was the first chance she had had to do for herself and to go over the happenings of the day. The highlight was seeing her husband off on his usual three to four-day crab fishing trip. It seemed normal enough, for the scene had played out many times before.

The calmness at the narrow entrance of the tiny river port beckoned and promised a good weather trip. That was earlier, when the sky was bright. Now, there was a high, thin, gray haze, along with unusual warm in the winter air, and a deathly stillness in the trees. If one had had time to think about it, these were all warnings of a storm. But it was only now, with cocoa in hand, that she could appreciate the signs and work herself into a state of apprehension. Part of the machinery that had made him go had been a reasonable weather report. That had changed drastically.

As she sat there, the first edges of the storm began to show the signs of its size and strength against the coast and against the house. A premonition of disaster invaded her thoughts, her very being. In her head, she argued against it saying, "How silly I am. It's happened before, worrying myself for days only to find he's anchored up somewhere, or gone to another port. After all, he's been fishing for most of his life.

Still, it makes me so angry to be put through this. I could bang the bastard on the head with his own arm! And then he walks in and with a smile says 'Hi honey! I'm home!' Oh God! Please, please don't let this be the one! If I lost him, I'd have nothing left!"

From where the house stood, she could hear the surf begin to pound the rocky shore with a vengeance. The wind rattled the loose bits and pieces around the house. It moaned through the swaying trees, heralding that the storm had come.

Unsatisfied and unconvinced, she went to bed. Despite the increasing cold that came with the wind, inside the house heat was building, gathering strength from itself, gaining a weight that was pressing down, almost smothering the restless, sleeping family. As the woman's body became still, she began to drift down with the drug of the heat to permanent sleep.

~

The Blessed Redeemer cruised smoothly, with a slow, easy roll, a slight rise and fall over the long, slow swells, like a head lying lightly on a lover's breast, rising and falling with gentle breaths. The man sat in the cubbyhole of the pilot house, leaning against the wall, with his arm on the windowsill to support his chin. One foot was braced against the shelf below the steering wheel, housing the autopilot, which held the small thirty-eight-foot boat on course.

The crewman put the supplies away and went out on deck to check the lashings on the last of the crab traps. They were to be placed with the others on the grounds off the next port, about 100 nautical miles or so up the coast. Going into the cabin, the crewman leaned against the far wheel dash and, looking out through the forward windows, he said, "Well, if we didn't have to run the gear, I'd say, let's wait a day. It looks to me like the shit's coming."

"Yep, me, too," the man replied. "But we have to go. And maybe with luck, we'll do the job before it hits. Why don't you go down and take the first bunk watch?"

"OK," the crewman said. "But I'll bet you after it hits, the God-damned weather people will catch up with it and tell us what we already know. Then, he stooped down and crawled through a hole in the dash to the small two-bunk fo'c'sle.

The man looked out thoughtfully at the darkening horizon, reading all the signs. He concluded it was a southerly, which was normal this time of year. However, he knew that to produce, you worked and took what came. If it was real bad, you went in.

He was a tough one, with sharp features, of average height, and lean but wiry. He was a natural fisherman and one of the top high-liners of the area. That's how he got the boat he had. The fish-buyers had given it to him. He had lost his own new boat and, of course, he had to pay for this one out of his catches.

The new boat he had lost was a true Jonah. It kept breaking down and he couldn't make a full trip. He wasn't making payments. He never thought it would happen to him. Instead of working hard, losers gave "bad luck" as the excuse for why they didn't make it. But he had worked hard and struggled all his life. Starting with a skiff as a kid, he labored and stayed out when others were in. He worked step by step, getting better and larger boats, until he could build his own, one of the first, truly big, modern fishing vessels of that port.

He was proud of his boat, and maybe, just a little bit arrogant. But despite all his efforts, he couldn't get fishing time with it. First, it took too long to build and cost more than expected. Then, when he tried to fish it, one major thing at a time would break down at strategic intervals, and no money was brought in. One of the last straws was when he was lifting the anchor in medium wind to go fish with the other boats and his winch tore from the deck and jammed against the bow bulwarks. He lost heart then, and let the bank foreclose.

He was not willing to take full responsibility for his failure to have caught the blatantly poor workmanship in construction. He couldn't admit the he'd allowed himself to be taken for so long. So, he ate it. After this experience, he began to see that his earlier attitude towards others and their circumstances were hard and unforgiving, and did not allow for things or happenings that were beyond one's capacity to control. He wanted to atone, but how?

Then again, he wasn't really sure what he should atone for? Still, he resolved that he would atone. He would atone through visible signs, like those of old, who sent sacrifice to God by flame, a flame that told, without words, how faithful and pious one was. He grew a beard and became more open about his fundamentalist faith. As a demonstration of thoughtful change, he renamed the boat for all to see. He was starting again with the "Blessed Redeemer."

In spite of this, he didn't feel complete or secure. His production was the same as in his best days, but his heart wasn't in it. The longer he had the boat, the more he wanted out of the business. Impatiently, he put it up for sale, but it was the wrong time of year. There was one person who was interested, but he wouldn't be able to buy it 'til spring. So, the man would have to put in one more winter crab-season, before he could safely get out. As he awakened from his thoughts, safety began to cross his mind. The boat was beginning to react to the rising wind and sea.

He noted that it was late afternoon. He was surprised how fast the time had passed, and how swiftly the storm was pressing down on them. At least, he thought, it was on the stern and they could slide if they were careful. The visibility decreased, with heavy, low, overcast rainsqualls up to five square miles in diameter.

Devastating 40-knot gusts dotted the area like mortar fire in advance of an approaching army, softening and demoralizing its enemy.

He reached over and tuned his radio to the weather channel. With sinking spirit, he listened to the new report, which was dramatically changed from the one he'd heard earlier. He now truly wished he could have waited, but they were too far along to turn back. He awakened his crewman, who came out instantly, immediately aware of what was happening. Both would be on watch that night. They had but an hour until complete darkness. The sea had caught up with the steady 30-knot winds. The waves had already been whipped to a significant size, but now, 40 to 50-knot gusts worked in concert with the severe and stronger currents of the area. Darkness would surely bring the ultimate test for the small, heavily laden vessel.

The boat slid down the forward side of a sharp swell, gained speed and, with the force of the wind and sea, was turning to a slight angle, when the crest of the wave behind pushed down and broke over the running stern. Just then, another wave dropped a log, large and heavy, into a slingshot-like trough. The log came up butt first, with all its buoyant force. It came up and the boat came down. And then, they met.

In the cabin, cannon noise couldn't have been louder. The shuddering shock made the men stagger and threw drawers and their contents into every corner. Tools and oilcans clanged against the engine. The boat stopped. The deck was awash. The seas were rolling and hitting the side sharply, like sledge hammers pounding a heavy steel drum. Just short of panic, the two men looked at the water filling the forecastle and engine room. The inner skin of planking sheltered from view the true extent of the damage to the outer shell of planks. Even so, the men could see that the end of the Blessed Redeemer was just minutes away.

The man, accepting the facts, barked the orders "Turn the deck lights on! Get the raft out!" Then, he shouted into the radio, "Mayday! Mayday!" The coastguard answered instantly. The man gave his position and said, "My boat is sinking fast. We hit a log! My deckhand and I will be in a raft. Please come quick! Over!"

"Mayday! Received you! What are your sea conditions?" the coastguard replied.

"Back! Severe weather! Winds..." Just then, the man was interrupted. The water rose over the batteries, shorting out the electrical system. "Fifty knots!" was shouted into a dead mike. The man went out onto the watery deck to help with the raft. His knee boots were filled with shockingly icy water. The cold wind, full of spray, stung his face. The raft was inflated and tied to the lee rail, as the winds screamed and pushed with incredible force.

In spite of the heavy winter clothing and foul weather skins the men wore, their senses were attuned, not to the scene, boat, sky or water, but to the surrounding, solid cold. Their minds retreated and their bodies reacted instinctively. With the boat settling deeper, the man jumped into the raft. Turning to help his crewman, he realized the line had to be cut. In the same instant, the crewman went to get a knife from the cabin. It was a command and an action defying all explanation. The raft, tugging to be free, seemed so near. The crewman grabbed the line and cut. There was a second's hesitation. Their eyes met, then realization. The line was jerked from the crewman's hand. The boat was now sinking. The raft was still close.

The man shouted, "Jump!" The water, numbingly cold, took the crewman's breath away; his clothes, heavy, dragged his movements into a nightmare. The distance between them increased. There was nothing the man could do. All he could see were the large, round eyes that dominated all else. They were like the eyes of a puppy that had been kicked by its master. There was no accusation, only shocked surprise, apprehension, and a moment of hope, as the crewman tried to make it.

The sharp sea rose up and washed over him. Although they were a large trough apart, one wailing, the other coughing and spitting water, they were two minds in tune, bound by one objective. A wall of water rose up and curled over, then licked the crewman down. The man, for all time, lost completely his willful ego, and any semblance of being the manipulator of his own destiny. The thick, fast-moving grey clouds changed rapidly into night. The man was now utterly alone.

~

Five miles downwind from the target, the large Coast Guard copter lined up for its first run They flew as close to the surface as they dared, in order to make use of the powerful spotlight. Forty-five minutes after the call, and fifteen minutes after dark, the 'copter was directly over the location given in the mayday call. Coming around and setting up for a planned search pattern, the 'copter was given an exceptionally heavy buffeting. The co-pilot, with a slight quiver to his voice, said, "Jesus, Cap! That gust must have been over 60 knots!"

The navigator shouted out a new course and then said, "Yes! The instruments have shown no less than 45 knots all the way out!"

"That spotlight isn't good for shit," the co-pilot yelled. "It's just bouncing off all that crap out there. I can't see a thing!"

One of the two young crewmen at watch through the side ports shouted to no one in particular, "I think it's hopeless! There is so much white water down there, rain and glare! You can't tell one from the other! And besides, it's as cold as hell!"

The medical corpsman watching next to him said, "Well, I know for a fact, with this wind, that water down there will be a lot less than 46 degrees. So, if those two guys were in the water, they wouldn't last thirty minutes."

With five hours flying time, and hoping for a break in the weather, or visibility, they looked and flew like a tiny thorn, trying to penetrate the hide of an elephant. The storm, unaware of the Herculean effort being made to cut into its pores, went blithely about its business. With no letup in the struggle, the 'copter was forced to break off the search and made it back with a bare reserve. All the pilot could do was hand in his report.

At about 5 minutes to 1:00 a.m., the Coast Guard officer sat down at his desk. Squaring the phone in front of him, he wiped the sweat from his hands on the legs of his pants. Then, he leaned back to compose himself. He thought over what he was going to tell the fisherman's wife, and what information he had to get from her.

With the looks of it and new information on this storm, it could last for days. He needed to know what kind of emergency gear her husband and his crewman had, in order to make a fair estimate of their chances for survival, and how long they would look for them. "Her name. Mrs. Nicholson. Must remember that," he told himself. He reviewed once more the report in front of him. He leaned forward, the nervous sweat making his shirt stick to his back. He noted it was one in the morning. He took the phone, dialed the number, and then waited for someone to answer.

~

The little ball of consciousness, diminishing as it proceeded down the narrow, dimly lit corridor, pinpointing into a blank spot, became aware of a disturbance. The habits of years took over, like stepping out the back door to go shopping and then hearing the phone and, not having the will to let it go, dashing back to answer it, thinking "I must answer that phone before leaving." Reluctantly, and with great effort, consciousness trudged back up to the seat of complete awareness and command. Except for the insisting phone, all the outer sensory organs were numb and sweaty, retreating from the now terrible heat. But the brain, trying to awaken from drowning in the raindrop-like pinpricks of pain, pain from trying to breathe, was sounding the alarm for immediate attention and correction. The command went out to the phone receiver, the nearest and easiest alarm signal.

"Oh...What is it?" the woman asked. The male voice on the other end answered, "Mrs. Nicholson? Sorry to have awakened at this time. I'm Lt. Cooper of the Coast Guard Command District 12."

Her heart and stomach scrunched up. A new alarm sounded in her brain. As the impersonal official droned on, something about the boat sinking and the men abandoning it and needing to know what kind of raft they might have gotten into, the words seemed to jumble up. Her consciousness locked onto the smoke pouring into her room, along the ceiling. A dancing light reflected from down the hall. A crackling roar registered along with the words, "They are lost at sea."

Almost at the same moment, she cried out, "The house is on fire!"

The house was on fire! Screaming, "Children! Children," she jumped into action. The front and service side of the house were in total flames. She could not remember how or in what order she carried the youngest and the two older ones. With blankets wrapped around them, their hair plastered to their heads, rain dripping from their noses, all of them sobbing and stunned, they watched the 50-year old house, with all their worldly goods, burn from the inside out, like it had been built of straw.

The Fire Chief found them wrapped and shivering in their blankets, about 60 yards or so out back, at the edge of the trees. They were all struck dumb by the event. Not yet aware of her double blow, he went to them and put his arm around the woman's shoulders. Even though she couldn't comprehend yet, he said, as gently as he could, the kindest words that could have possibly been said at that moment. "I'm here now, Hon. Just let go. I will take care of everything. You just come along with me."

On the way to the hospital, the Chief called ahead on his radio so all would be ready. As they drove, the woman began to mumble and talk in tearful fits. By the time they reached the hospital, the Chief had heard enough of the story to realize the true magnitude of the disaster. And he knew this family. He considered them friends. He knew the fisherman's best friend and his family. They were a fishing family as well. He called them immediately and told the story and asked what the Coast Guard needed to know.

The friend explained that the lost boat did have a new type of raft that helped against exposure, and he agreed to continue coordinating with the Coast Guard. The best friend also agreed to a course of action to take care of the woman and her children.

By about 10 o'clock the next morning, the friend had collected some clothes and picked up the kids. They were doing OK. He took them to his home, where there was warmth and comfort and family. The woman remained sedated at the hospital and would be taken to his home later that day. The friend then went to meet with the Fire Chief. There were still many things that needed doing, and people to see.

By about 4 o'clock that afternoon, just about everybody in the town knew what had happened. The foundation was laid for things to be prepared. The storm, in all its fury, raged on. By evening, the woman was brought to the friend's house and was comforted as best they could. With a sleeping pill, she would make it through the night.

The next two days seemed like a blur, as so many people came by. With so much visiting, and the news of all the wonderful things that were happening for her, with all the love and concern, the woman was spellbound. It seemed that the fishermen had gotten up a collection of about $2,000 or so. The townspeople gathered all the basics, including food and clothes, and all they could think of for living. They arranged for a good, used trailer that would be on permanent loan from the local RV dealer. By the third day, the trailer was packed and placed at the trailer park.

That evening at dinner, it was decided that the next day, her friends would keep the kids, while the woman went to the trailer for the day and night, just to be alone for a bit. That very evening the storm eased off. The News reported the storm as the worst in years, but that it was now passing and the Coast Guard could and would renew their search the next day.

The following day was the fourth since the fire. About mid-morning, as her friend was driving the woman to the trailer for her alone-time, the sun appeared in half the sky, warming the cold, damp ground. They could just see the back of the storm disappearing to the east. In the western half of the sky, a few scattered rain clouds were trailing along, lightly washing up.

On their arrival at the trailer, the friend escorted her to the door. They stood awkwardly for a quiet moment. With a fierce, tearful emotion, the woman hugged him with such force it took his breath away. Then she ran inside and slammed the door. The friend stood for a moment, understanding, though not fully, and then quietly left.

Inside, without thinking, the woman went to the nearest bedroom and lay down and cried. Then, she dozed a little, and rested. When she awoke, she began to look around. She was in the end bedroom. "It must be the "master," she thought because it had a queen-sized bed. There was also a bathroom, fully stocked. She washed her hands and rinsed her face. She went to the kitchen and saw that it had a large refrigerator and, of course, a stove.

"Oh," she exclaimed, "an electric coffee maker!" Looking through the well-stocked cupboards, she found coffee and prepared a pot. A small bookshelf divided the kitchen from the living-room. The living room had two easy chairs, a small coffee table, a couch that would fold out into a bed, and even a small T.V. There was another small bathroom, which she thought was for the kids. There was also a wardrobe and a small linen closet, both full. Then came the last bedroom. "Oh God," she exclaimed again, "there are bunk beds!"

Going back into the living room, she turned on the heat, took her jacket off, put it on the kitchen table, and then poured a cup of coffee and sat down in an easy chair. She took a sip and set the cup on the lamp table. Some of the things were new. Most were used but in such good shape, they could have been new. She thought to herself, "This is better than the old house. We'll all be so cozy."

Then, she began to sob again. She rubbed her temples. After a bit, from where she sat, she looked at each and everything. As she looked, there seemed to her a glow all around. For the first time, she began to realize, "All those people. All that love." And she began to see what she had always taken for granted. She had been brought to this place as a child, grew up, married, had children, and never traveled very far.

She'd never thought deeply about any of it. It seemed to her that all she had done was drift through life with her eyes half-closed. But now, thinking over the key points of the last four days, she sensed the presence of God. She saw the proof of that Presence through the actions and love of the people of her community, so evident in the things around her. She shuddered at the thought, but now, even if her man was never found, she knew, with all this love and support at her side and given a little time, she could make it.

It was dark outside and she had not moved for hours. Then, a loud knock woke her up. It was the trailer park manager with a message. With beating heart, she opened the door. "Evening," he said, and handed her a piece of folded paper. He added, "Your friend called this in."

She took the paper and read, "The Coast Guard called. Your husband was plucked up this afternoon, a hundred miles out, by a ship going into Eureka. He's well, but he was alone. Have gone up to get him. Be back some time in the morning."

Tears were running down her cheeks. "You going to be all right?" the manager asked. "Yes! Yes! Thank you," she responded, wiping her tears.

The manager took his leave saying, "Yep, well! If you need anything, just call. Good night."

She closed the door to prepare herself. She knew it would be the longest night of her life, but it would be one of the happiest. As she settled down, there was a great, almost unbearable swelling in her chest. She heard herself say out loud, "No more will I drift through life—not with what I've just received!"

~

During the six-hour ride aboard the ship to its berth, the man was fed. He had a shower and his clothes were washed and dried. By the time a Coast Guard officer picked him up and took him to the offices, he was in pretty good shape, considering the ordeal. He would never forget the last moments of the accident.

After he gave them a report, they took him to a room with a cot and he slept. He'd been dozing for a couple of hours, when his friend came in and sat beside him. They touched each other's arms for a brief moment. As the man started to rise, his friend put a hand to his shoulder saying, "Wait." Stiffening, the man thought, "No more." And then, his friend told him the story of the phone call, the fire, and all the rest.

The whole picture flashed before the man's eyes at once. He thought of what could have been had he delayed his departure. If he had been home that night, the whole family could have gone up in smoke. If his boat hadn't gone down, and the call hadn't been made, he could have lost his family, and he would have been alone.

He would never know if the loss of his deckhand was an accident, or meant to be. But now, he accepted that it was beyond his understanding. He felt, as he got up to go, that truly God had spoken. He was glad to be alive. He was now able to go home, to be wherever his family was.

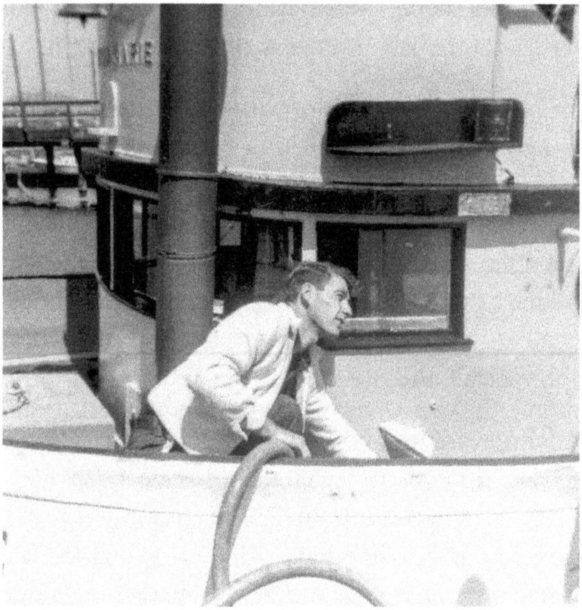

1964 Sausalito. Norman fueling the *Thea Marie*, his first boat.

SHORTY

1981

*T*he man was short, not much taller than my wife, who is 5' 2". Not many knew his real name. Short he is, so "Shorty" it was.

His blue Levis, faded and well worn, always neat and clean, covered a lean and wiry frame. Straight raven-black hair topped a brown and weathered-looking face. The thin-lipped slash of a mouth, one side of which he used for his hand-rolled cigarette, the other side for talking. That mouth showed the weight life had put upon him.

What drew me to him were his laugh lines, pointing to the humor in his pale blue eyes. It was his eyes that showed who he was, that he didn't take life's hard knocks, or himself, all that seriously.

The times that I thought of how he looked and what he radiated, I couldn't help but picture what a true, old-time cow-puncher he "musta" been.

Alas, nothing so romantic. He was, like me, a fisherman.

It was an early June of a typical salmon season, which at that time started on April 15th.

On a fairly decent trip, just a day or two from being completed, the wind came up with force, and a storm behind it. I ended the trip early by going into a nearby small fishing port, about 100 miles north of Frisco. While the wind blew, I cleaned up and had a day of waiting.

Shorty was at the café where all the fishermen hung out and the only one, by the way, having lunch. Not having seen him for a year, which is the way with most troll fishermen, I had lunch with him. We talked about lousy weather, lousy fishing, lousy politicians, how lousy it's been in general, and fishing gear and technique, the only things that weren't lousy.

After lunch and a lot of coffee, I asked him, "What's going on?

"Well," he says, "I finally got my new engine."

"Great, what kind is it?" was my next question

"Well, it's a rebuilt Jimmy diesel. You want to come see it?" Shorty asked.

"Sure!" I replied.

In no time we were on his thirty-six-foot boat, in a cubby hole of a cabin. With the floorboards out of the way, him sitting with legs dangling in what there was of an engine room and me, squatting, we looked at the bright, clean engine. We were like two kids contemplating the value of their favorite shooting marbles.

He told me that he'd just made his first trip with it, and what a pleasure it had been compared to the old one he'd been nursing for so long. I asked him how come he didn't put it in before the season.

"Well" he said, "I was afraid I'd lose part of that April run. You know how good that run is most of the time."

"You bet it is!" I agreed.

"So I left it for May, which is a lousy month," Shorty explained.

"Yeah. You're right about that, too," I said.

"As it was, I lost a couple days that first run," he remarked thoughtfully.

It was then that I noted two fresh scars on the side of his neck, partly covered by a neckerchief.

"How's that?" I asked.

"Well," he says, "it was opening morning, and I came down early to check things out.

With the engine warming up, I get down in there and grease up the fittings on the line shaft. When I go to get out, my rain slicker (like a dummy I still had it on) got caught in the belts."

"Oh Jesus!" I exclaimed.

"Yeah, you bet!" he laughed. "They pulled me down so fast I didn't have time to blink. Well, with my body jammed up to those pulleys, it stopped that poor old, wore out, goddamn engine, dead as hell. There I was, with my right arm twisted useless behind my back, two cracked ribs and a cracked collar bone. The slicker twisted up around my neck, making these two cuts that dripped my blood into the bilge. I was locked up tighter than dog shit in a garbage can!"

He paused. My stomach scrunched up just hearing of it.

Then, I said "Well, damn-it man! How the hell did you get out?"

Shorty continued. "Well, there I was, resting and half out, with my nose lying on that greasy engine mount, when all of a sudden, I hear engines revving up and guys running across MY boat to leave!"

"Didn't ya holler?" I asked.

"They couldn't have heard me with all the noise." Shorty answered. "Besides, I couldn't make a sound anyway."

"Go on!" I encouraged.

"Well, I got to thinkin' while I was lying there and couldn't move, all those bastards were going out there to get my share of fish. Shit! It made me so mad that if I could I woulda' spit. Anyway, my left arm was free, and don'tcha know, my knife was in my right pocket. Christ, I had a hell of time! I couldn't get my arm in front of me because of the belts. Finally, I twisted my hips so that with my arm behind me I could get the knife with my fingers. Well from then on I was in 'em. I opened it with my teeth, and cut myself out."

All I could do was squat there with my legs going to sleep and my mouth hanging open, as Shorty went on with his story.

"I didn't know how long it took me, but when I got onto the dock, it wasn't quite dawn and everybody was gone. It was too early in the morning for a "mayday" to the buyer; the office was still locked up. And by now I really didn't feel so well, so I thought I better get to the hospital. I got into the local buyer's dock car. Of course my right arm was so numb I couldn't use it but I managed anyway. With only a few close calls and one dented fender, I got to Santa Rosa, about 20 miles away. I checked myself in and after a day I'm all patched up and feeling good, so I checked out and made it back for the third day's fishing."

"Wow! What an experience!" I exclaimed. "It's a good thing you didn't change engines."

"Yeah," he laughs. After a moment he caressed the top of his new engine. "Ya know," he said, "if I'd put that thing in before the season and got caught like I did, with all its power, that bastard woulda' been the death of me."

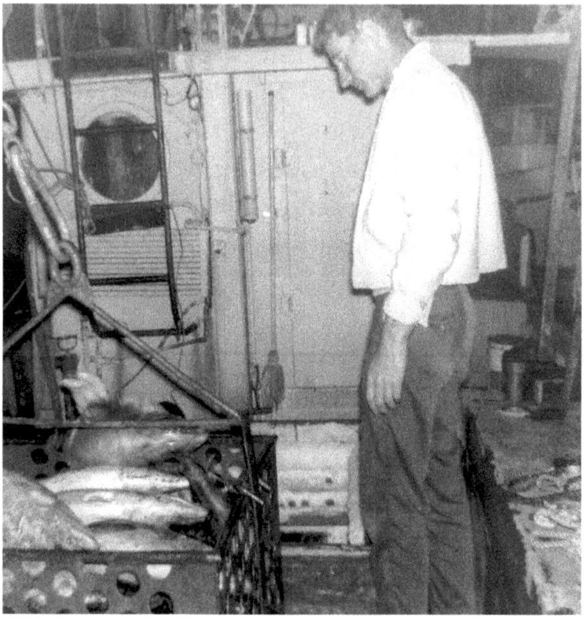

1964. Norman aboard the *Thea Marie* preparing to offload the trip's catch.

ONE'S DATE WITH MORE THAN COULD BE HANDLED

May 1978

There was a man, with a dark, curly beard whose large, beefy body, a bit loose, had been built by meat, potatoes and lots of beer. A wife and child gave foundation to his dream—to be his own man. Fishing was to be the means, so he sought a big boat on which to live off the sea. Fishing was to be the means. A small, cheap boat was what he could afford. With minimum effort, on weekends and vacations, during good weather and with bits of lines and hooks, he caught sufficient fish. When the wind came a-courting and the sea reacted, harbor and home were but an hour or so away.

Contentment was not on the table when he saw larger, long-range vessels come in with good catches, their skippers and crews sporting knowing smiles of satisfaction and relief. His eyes seem closed to troubles, broken trips and poor seasons. With beer in hand and good explanations, he talked, planned, and described what he could do with a bigger boat. And so a larger vessel was sought.

After selling his house and going into hock, he bought a boat, of medium-size, older than most and thoroughly used. They looked, he with bright-struck eyes and she with some misgivings, at his dream come true. He got a crewman who said he was experienced.

The man and woman, with their baby in a basket, went to work. The baby, shunted to shade or sun, its needs attended by one and all, was tickled and poked. Its responses brightened the moment. Eating was like a picnic on the sunny back deck. When cloudy or cool, they used the bench and table in the tiny galley, with an oil stove to keep them warm. As each day went by, the rusty, torn and blistered skin of the boat was sanded smooth and painted. Crude on the bilge from years of the engine's oily drips was scraped away. In fact, all that could be done with just muscle and sweat was done. So, the boat looked like it might go another round with sea and season. The wife's earlier fears were dulled by the boat's gloss.

The first trip of twenty days was all set. The day was clear, bright and still. The sea's slow, gentle pulse lured him out. This was the moment he had dreamed of and worked for—the perfect moment full of expectation and hopefulness. The whole season lay just ahead. The sea's gifts are exalting moments, sparingly granted. The payment is gruelingly extracted.

He was now on the high seas with a vessel that was small. Even though it was larger than the last, it could barely compare to the lifeboats of larger ships. For the time of year, good weather was only about twenty knots. The motion was continuous and bruising; simply taking a shit was a chore. It was all one could do to hang on and keep from getting wet. All weak and tired things that were essential for this game began to break down. Luckily, enough fish were caught to pay for repair and to outfit again.

After several more attempts to break even, the wife took a job due to pressure from payment deadlines. His timing was off and he went out in bad weather when the fishing was poor. More things were breaking down and the weather put the boat to the test. At these times he would have to come in, but it was good to get away from where he been. With beer in hand he waited for repairs. Then it was time to go out again. He would bemoan his luck to any who would listen, especially the repairman, who had heard it all before.

The more he tried the more he failed because he could not afford to replace, only repair. He worked as hard in port, crying over his beer, as he did fighting the ocean and the condition of his boat. His energy and judgment were going fast. He reasoned that with just a little more physical effort, hopefully the next good moment would surely come.

Out at sea, there was a tease of good weather and fine fishing. Then a storm came up that most fishing boats could take as matter of course. But it struck his boat a mortal blow and a seam opened in the hull. With all his pumps continually working, along with some portable ones donated by other concerned captains, he made it to port. Good fishing nearby lured the main body of the fleet to the same area, and the boats already in port were demanding facilities and services because of the escalating storm. With everyone trying to outdo each other telling how bad it had been for them, his troubles, no matter how severe, got lost. The man's anger, frustration and depression were almost complete. No one was listening.

He found a fisherman-diver waiting out the storm. He had equipment on board his small, versatile boat to patch the leaks as best he could in the murky harbor waters. Of course, it was difficult to do the job properly. The section needed to be rebuilt. The diver and others said a dry dock was needed. They suggested a cannery could front the money for the repair. But he wouldn't and couldn't take on the weight of more debt. Besides, he now needed only one pump to keep the leak well in hand.

He decided to leave with the change of weather. His deck hand was experienced enough to recognize the risk and quit. The man understood and accepted the deckhand's resignation, but he didn't want to be alone. He hired an inexperienced, young fellow off the street. After all, if things did go well, he would be needed. And, go well they did. With fair weather and good fishing the fleet in general was about to have what looked like the fastest trip of the season. All feelings were running "high"; you could almost touch them when the men talked to each other on the radio.

Then a short, fast-moving, violent storm came in the evening. It would be gone by morning. All that could be done was to hang on. But to the man, his crew and the boat, it was like a short uppercut to the chin of a worn-out boxer, putting him right out of the fight. About one o'clock in the morning, with the wind screaming in the rigging and a heavy overcast that made the night black, all that could be seen was the close white of cresting waves. They rolled and smacked into the boat and filled the deck with water. The man managed to holler for help on the radio. When asked what the matter was, he replied, "I have been up for hours trying to keep the water out and now it's just gotten out of hand!" He said he needed help badly and that he was so tired. So tired he couldn't do much more.

By then all the boats nearby were awake. They heard, "Oh God! The engine just shifted!"

There was a moment of silence. Then he said, "I'm so tired. I'm going to lie down and go to sleep."

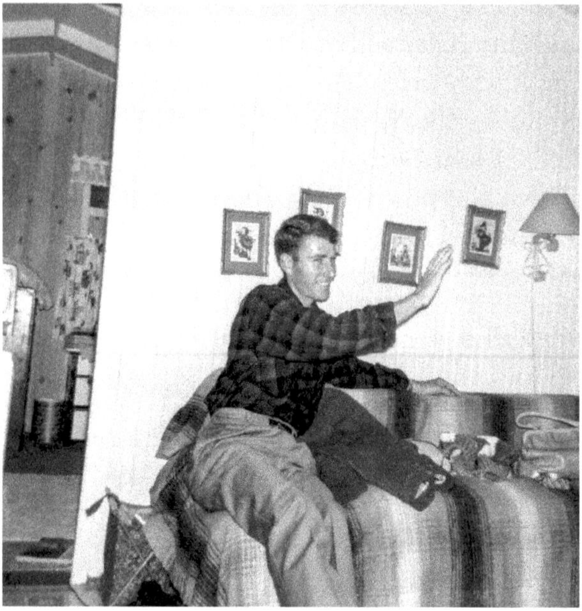

1964. Norman in his house in Sausalito telling stories at the end of the season.

A LITTLE EXPERIENCE I ONCE HAD

Late 1960s

Coming into Eureka from a salmon trip, and having been the max' time from home, I had this pounding urge demanding that I get back as soon as possible. No plan for twenty-four hours, to hell with that! The "Great American Dog (the Greyhound Bus)" was running all night, so away I went. It was just an hour and a half cold wait at the main depot. To pass the time, I started wandering around to amuse myself, looking at all the interesting characters in various stages of conscious. It then I felt a sudden need to take a shit.

Up a flight of stairs and around a corner was the place. I stepped into the room, though a large swinging door, bruised but painted a catchy green. With the low wattage the place had a drab, cheap, well-used look about it. Just straight on was a wall dividing the room, with mirrors and washbasins on both sides. To the right were all the urinals and pay toilets.

With a little jog to the left, you could walk on down between the washbasins and the free toilet booths. There I headed, all the time, while out of the corner of my right eye checking myself out of the mirrors till I got to the stall of my choice, hoping it would have toilet paper. To the left in the corner just beyond the catchy green door was the shoe shine stand, a four-seater, and there sat the shoe shine man. He was straight out of a Shirley Temple movie, short, round, middle aged, with a round face and a bald shiny head ringed with white kinky hair like an old Roman senator. He carried permanent press work cloths and wore a tan apron tied at the waist and with polish stains. His shirt sleeves were rolled half way up, exposing his dark brown, round forearms. He sat with hands clasped together, his elbows restin' on his knees, just looking. Next to him was the blackest string bean of a guy. He wasn't too tall and was neatly dressed with tight dark pants and vest, worn over a loose bright shirt and a string tie. He wore a dark derby hat with a tiny bright feather in the band and sat in the same position as his friend, sitting, lookin' an' waitin'. Both of them looked for all the world like two black crows, sitting on a fence, waiting for the farmer to get out of the corn patch.

Down that row of wash basins, right across from the second to the last free toilet stall with its door gone, was a little old completely bald black man, wearing a neat looking light-colored suit that could have stood a little cleaning and pressing. He had a bit of a wizened look, hooded eyes, and he dabbed a wet, cool paper towel to his face.

Good, God! His face was beat to a pulp. The hooded eyes were from being swollen half-shut. His cheeks glistened red and raw, the lower lip protruding a half-inch or so was split and purple. There were drops of blood half wiped up on the front of his white shirt. Coming nosily in almost immediately behind me was a tidy bearish man of medium height, with a round friendly baby face, beaming white. I moved aside to let him in. He jogged to the left and then, taking us all in at once, them and me, standing there with my hands in my heavy jacket pockets, making my six foot four 180-pound frame look even bigger. There we were, just looking, but right at him. I don't know what he thought, because I didn't know what to think either, but all the blood left his face as he instantly froze. "Oh Jesus," couldn't of been plainer on his face than if he had shouted it.

The old black man while looking at him, started to go through his pockets. Not finding what he wanted, he turned and with a painful shuffle and went right up to the new guy. With his sorrowful face just inches away, he look's him straight in the eye and said, "Has you a cigarette?"

"Yeah, yeah," out the words came. Nobody could have answered faster.

The old man ever so slowly took a cigarette from the jittering pack and put it to his lips. Then, while still toe-to-toe, he went through his pockets. Nothing. Then he says, "Has you a match?"

"Yeah, yeah," faster than a speeding bullet the lit match was at the end of that cigarette. A couple of puffs and then the old man painfully made his way back to the wash basin across from the free toilet stall with no door. Freed, the man turned and boy did he move. And that goddamn catchy green door caught him square with a bang. "Christ," was knocked out of him. A silly sheepish grin blazed to us all. He bounced and then slid for the opening, like a billiard ball going straight for the side pocket, and then he was gone.

Just as I'm about to wake myself up and go for a toilet, the skinny dandy jumps down from the stand and starts a shuffling strut towards me. About halfway, as he was coming, he said, "Hey man, you got"…

I snap to and cut him off with my deepest voice. "Don't bug me! I'm just here to just take a shit!"

"Ok! Ok! Big man, take it easy," and he went back to his stand as I went right, to the pay toilets.

"Crap!" no quarter. "Goddamn, no-good pay toilets." Back I go, around the divider, past the two men just sitting and looking, down the aisle between the free toilet stalls and washbasins, taking a quick sly peek out of the corner of my right eye, past the old guy at his basin, standing across from the free open stall. Well at least it had some paper. Going in, I sat down, leaning forward so that I could keep watch. The old guy's legs were in the same place, the other two I couldn't see. Nothing changed.

Exasperated, the circulation in my legs was getting cut off. Just then in the stillness, there was a sudden loud plop! "Oh Well." Feeling a little silly, I flushed the toilet and straightened myself up. I went out to the basin next to the old guy still nursing that cigarette. As I washed my hands, I thought he might have been a little drunk too. Well he did look to be doing all right; gently patting his face with a cool wet paper towel. Trying to appear casual, I walked out, with just the slightest misstep right in front of the two who were looking and waiting. Quietly, I went down to the waiting room to finish my own waiting. "I betcha I fooled them. I bet they never guessed how nervous I was!"

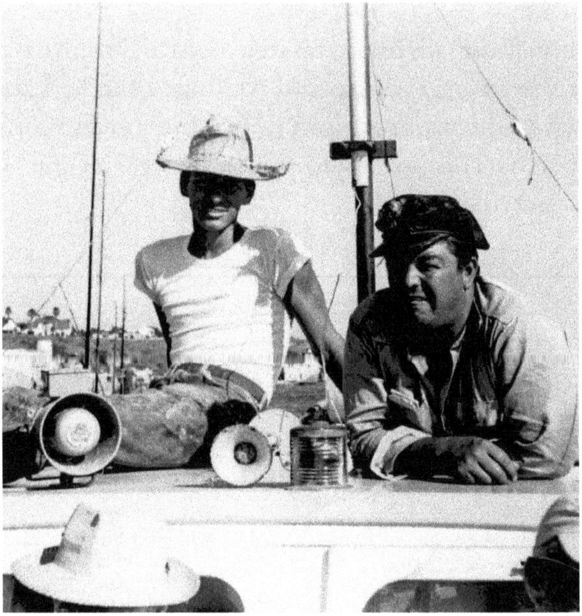

1950 Newport Beach. Norman age 14 with his first boss.

DOWN TO SEA IN LITTLE BOATS

1951

This story was narrated to Robbin La Vine, Norman's daughter in 2015. It was an assignment for an English class in High School and the first story he remembers writing. As Norm tells it, he handed the story in and his teacher was thrilled. She asked if she could keep it and he consented. He remembered the story well but never saw the document again.

My mother had a little cabin at a vacation village in Newport Beach, California. We stayed there every summer from the time I was eight. There were other families that came, as well. My mother visited with all her summer friends, and I would play with my summer friends. We swam, played on the sand and had a little rowboat with a motor. We explored the back bay where we played pirates and lay in the sun.

At age 15, my mother thought it was time for me to do something else. She drove me to the part of the Bay where people docked their commercial fishing boats, sports boats, and pleasure boats. She parked the car and told me to check things out.

It was afternoon. The commercial and sport boats were tied up. Deckhands were cleaning and skippers were overseeing the work. I asked if they needed help. Most weren't interested, but one was losing a deckhand. He told me to return the following morning and we'd give it a try. It was one of the sport vessels. Over time, I learned the ropes, how to clean fish, and earn tips from the customers.

One early morning as I was preparing for the day, the skipper arrived with an attractive young woman—his girlfriend. The girlfriend said she had a little charter boat that took six people and that is how she made a living. On days she didn't have a charter, she enjoyed a day off on her boyfriend's boat.

Once when the day was over, she helped me clean the fish. The work was quickly done, so we climbed up on top of the cabin with the captain, who was seated with his legs though the hatch and his feet on the steering wheel.

She turned to me and asked, "Do you have any girlfriends?"

"No." Then she asked if I had ever had a kiss. "No." She looked at me for a while. I felt shaken.

"Well," she said, "it's about time you get one!" She leaned in. My eyes were huge. Halfway towards me her eyes rose and there sat her boyfriend, my skipper, my boss, glaring at us. He didn't look happy.

She backed off saying, "Oh well, it don't matter," and turned the conversation to something else.

On returning to the dock, she stuck around to help clean up and prepare the boat for the following day. Then she and the skipper took off and I went home.

The next day, she had a charter and her boat was gone. After our own customers were taken care of, the fish cleaned, and the boat docked and readied for the following day, the skipper let me go. He said I wasn't a good deckhand and he'd found somebody else.

On my way home, I passed two commercial vessels tied together near the end of the dock. The skippers were prepping for the next trip. I asked if they needed help. The captain of the smaller vessel said "Yes! Come back tomorrow and we'll have work for you. Be ready to go out day after tomorrow."

When I got home, I told my mother that I lost my job but got another! This time I'd be a deckhand on a commercial vessel. The work would be different from what I had experienced before, and I would be at sea for about 10 days each trip.

My new captain's running partner had a crew that consisted of his children. There were three - a daughter of 15, a younger brother and the youngest, a sister.

We had a few trips before reaching near the end of the season. Then, a final trip was scheduled and away we went.

Halfway through the trip, the weather came up in a sudden squall of rough seas and strong winds. We were outside the Islands off Catalina. We went to a little harbor on the upper end of Catalina Island, to an anchoring cove. We anchored up, tied together, shared meals and waited out the storm. The following day, the sun came up and after breakfast, the young people decided to go swimming. Just within the harbor there was a sunken vessel. We took a little skiff, and with me at the oars, the four of us rowed over. We tied off to the top of the cabin and played there for hours, diving off the top of the heavy mast, which listed at a slight angle. The time slipped by and before long the running partner called his children home for food.

I manned the oars again. The eldest girl sat in the nose of the boat at my back, and the two younger ones sat in the stern in front of me. There was little room for all of us. In order for me to make a full sweep of the oars, the girl behind me adjusted her legs to give me room to row. As I leaned back and pulled on the oars, my torso had to pass between her parted knees. With each stroke of my body, her flesh just brushed my own.

The following morning our little fleet finished the trip and the season. When we returned to the docks and the mainland, before leaving I asked the daughter if I could have her number. She gave it to me and then we had to say "Goodbye." As I left, I began to feel a hint of what the sport-fishing captain's girlfriend was trying to show me.

Then, the summer was over. I helped my mother pack up the cabin at Newport and we returned to Highland Park, where we lived and where I went to school. After we were settled in, I wanted to call my summer friend, but in the flurry of the move, I had lost her number.

Oh well. So it goes, we go down to the sea in little boats.

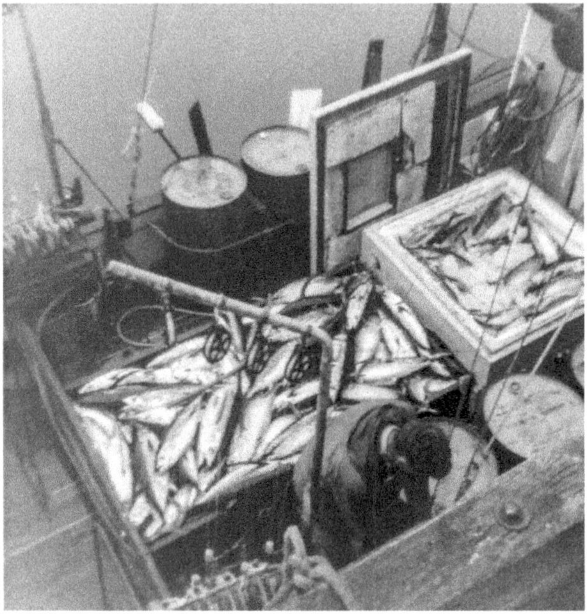

1964. Waiting to offload the catch.

A FULL HOLD AND A LOAD ON DECK

This story was dictated to Robbin La Vine in 2016, a family favorite that was never written down

When I was ten, I smoked my first tobacco. I lived on a dead-end street across from a graveyard where my friends and I hung out. We picked up cigarette butts off the street and packed them into corncob-bubble pipes. We crept onto the cemetery grounds to smoke, chat, and crouch behind tombstones.

By the time I was in my early teens, I was a full-time smoker. I went to school every day with a pack in my pocket. During breaks and recess, I'd sometimes step off school grounds for a smoke. After school, I'd light up a cigarette for the walk home. I was fifteen when my dad caught me with a pack in my socks. I wasn't much older when the school principal caught me smoking. They both told me it would hurt my health, but I ignored them. By the time I was in my mid-twenties, I was smoking two to three packs daily.

At thirty, I was married with a baby on the way, and getting sick in the winter. There was one stretch where I was sick for nearly six weeks straight. I spent most of that time in bed. It was so bad, I couldn't even smoke. I realized that smoking made me sick and I resolved to quit. Just to test myself, I kept a pack in my pocket. It took me eight months to realize that I was free and throw the pack away.

A year later, bad weather and an engine-part pushed me into port at Eureka, California. I was hanging with some buddies of mine at the local harbor coffee shop. We were shooting the breeze and enjoying coffee, when I noticed three guys walk into the shop, eyeballing all around. They sat at a table next to the window, a good spot from which to survey the action. It didn't take long before I realized one guy had stopped looking around and was staring straight at me. He was watching my every move. His scrutiny was obvious. I raised my hand and ran it through my hair. His eyes followed. "Hmmm…" I thought. I lowered my hand. My legs were spread, as I leaned back in my seat. I reached down between my legs and scratched. His eyes followed there, too. "Ah ha!" I thought and paid him no more mind.

A few minutes later I'd finished my cup and rose to leave. A couple of paces outside the coffee shop, I felt a tap on my shoulder. There was the guy, accompanied by his two friends. It was then that I realized my first impression was mistaken. This was different. I had the feeling this was going to be something special for me. It turned out that the men were casting for a television commercial. They were looking for the next guy to "walk a mile for a Camel," and they thought I was it.

They scheduled filming for the next day. They gave me a pack of Camels and I started smoking. I needed to regain the ease that I no longer had, in order to ensure I could smoke on screen. We set up in the woods with the big trees of the Pacific Northwest as a backdrop. For three days they filmed and I smoked. When we were done, I threw the last pack in the trash. But two days later they were back for a do-over. The film was too dark. Again, I smoked while I strolled on screen, this time with lights. I enjoyed the smoke curling out of my lungs. I took it as part of my job requirement for them. It was just for a couple of days. I had no problem quitting.

The whole episode took a little over a week. By the time we were done, my part came in. I fixed my engine and I was ready to go back out to sea. I couldn't help feeling that it was time well spent. The pay, including royalties, was equal to a full hold and a load on deck. What an easy trip!

Soon after my commercial aired, onscreen tobacco advertising was banned. My commercial was one of the last.

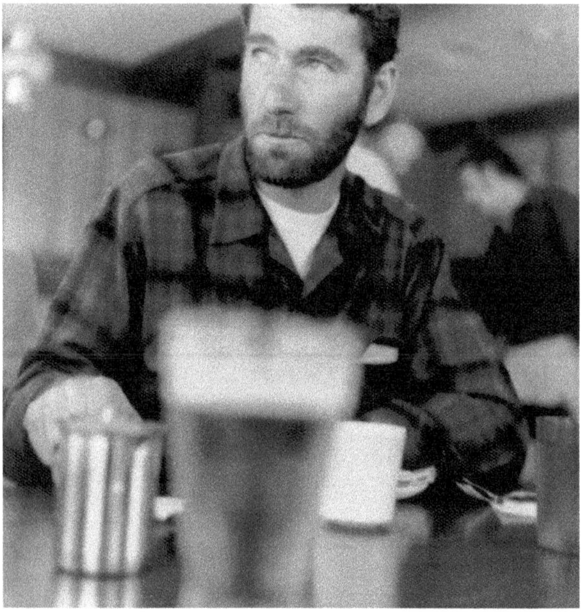

1974 Norman at a diner in Morro Bay.

GETTING ACQUAINTED WITH DOLPHINS

This story was dictated to Robbin La Vine in 2016, a long-time family favorite

I had just finished the last salmon trip and unloaded what I had at Sausalito, the closest fish-buying dock to the entry of San Francisco Bay. I needed to clean up, get ready for the first albacore trip, and get a little rest. One of my favorite chores is doing the laundry. I went over to the Laundromat, loaded the machine and sat on the bench to relax and read the paper. Then, in walked Peter.

Peter is of average height, has a stocky build, a friendly face and is very strong. After he filled his machine, he saw me, came over and sat down to visit. It sure was good to see him. Last year, his boat sank out from under him. The fleet first heard about it when he called "May-day!" over the radio. His boat was loaded and the rudderpost bearing was dry. That combination sunk his boat. I hadn't seen him since. I jumped up and exclaimed, "Peter! It's sure good to see you after what happened last year!"

He smiled at me. "Yeah," he said. "It's been a long time. I'm lucky to have this visit with you. And it's a damn good thing I had a lifejacket!"

I laughed. "Thank goodness! A lifejacket and fine weather. So what are you working with now?"

"Well, the fish buyer knew someone with a bigger boat, and it's got refrigeration. I can go out, and for albacore," he replied.

Of course, my next question was "Are you going to buy it?"

Peter's answer was, "No, I can't yet, but the share is great and the owner's a good guy."

"Well, that's great," I said.

Then we shifted in our seats and sat awhile. Finally, I asked, "So, what happened? What was it like in the water?"

With that, Peter began his story. "Well, I was lucky that the water was warm. But even so, the sun was almost down and I knew it would be dark soon. Then, the most fantastic thing happened. The sea was smooth and gentle and I could see a long distance. Up to the north, I began to see splashes and, as the splashes got closer, I recognized dolphins. There must have been about a hundred and I was in the middle of their path. Soon, I was surrounded! Their curiosity and gentleness was amazing. As each one had their turn to gently rub past and touch me, I did the same. I held out my hands and stroked them. It seemed like I was joining a family.

Some of them let me hold their dorsal fin and towed me around. It felt like this getting acquainted and playing went on for hours, but it probably wasn't more than one. Then, the sun went down and it was time for them to continue their trip."

"At that moment, there was a change in their movements, transforming into vibrations and sounds. It lasted a minute or two and then the main group continued on their trip. But they left behind five to guard me. During the night, they watched me close. If I fell asleep and my head would slip into the water, one of them would bump me and wake me up."

"At last, morning came and the conditions hadn't changed, thank goodness! The weather was calm and we were still together. During that time, my companions and I gently snuggled in turns, and at the same time, I would look over toward the horizon. During this time we had a few visitors. Luckily, they weren't the real aggressive kind. They were just blue sharks, reaching no more than 8 to 12 feet in length. But the dolphins butted them so hard, the sharks shot out of there as fast as they could."

"About noon the dolphins seemed to be getting aware of something and I caught their excitement. I began to look out around the horizon and saw a fishing boat coming down from the northwest. My pals and I jumped and splashed! They were doing most of the jumping! As the boat sailed closer I could see the skipper and his deckhand. They were waving back to us! In about two minutes, they were there and hauled me aboard. Once I was safe, the dolphins took off to catch up with their family."

"Oh Peter," I exclaimed, "what an incredible experience, and how lucky for you!"

Peter got a little quiet and finally he said, "Norman, you must know about the attitude the dolphins have toward us."

I was glad to tell him "Yep. Some time ago, my wife got a book from the library about the history of dolphins, clear back to ancient times. It told about the things that they have done for the individuals they've bumped into."

Peter seemed to have something important to share with me because he suddenly asked me, "Well, do you know what our God-damn government is doing with them?"

Peter was really angry now and he said, "The government and those Russian bastards are training dolphins to plant magnetic bombs on enemy ships. They're training them to be weapons. I'm so pissed off I can't stand it! The dolphins have been friendly to human beings. Can you imagine if the bomb got stuck in the holster? Even after it's planted to the hull, how long till it goes off? How will it affect them? Do you know that dolphins have bigger brains than we have? They are more aware of us than we are of ourselves. Believe me, I know! When we are on the sea and our boats sink, if they are near, they help us!"

TUG BOAT IRENE

This story was dictated to Robbin La Vine in 2016

It was just about the end of albacore season. I was trolling in from way off shore, heading into homeport and hoping for a last catch of fish to top off the load. About half way in, I saw a boat, drifting and bait fishing, slow and steady. My boat was of a similar size, with a small bait tank. I trolled all around, jigs out but no bites. I came closer, but still no luck. Then I saw her. She was fishing with a deckhand, also a woman, both taking turns throwing bait then hauling in the fish. They were large women and looked strong, but the one, she was taller than the other. She was fantastic. That was the first time I saw Irene.

I hadn't got one bite on the jigs. The fish were down deep and only came up for live bait. So following the example of the two women, I brought the jig lines in and stopped the boat about a quarter mile off to their side. My crewmate was also a woman, my wife Angela. She had a small bait scoop and started throwing bait out just right. With me using the jig pole, we started getting fish, albacore, big ones, about 30 to 50 pounds each. Time was passing and the fish were still coming steady. Angela could not manage to lift the fish on her own so it was up to me to haul them in and her to throw the bait. After a while, I felt my strength falter and a couple of times, I fell. My honey called over, "Norman! Stop and rest a moment!" All I could say was, "They're biting. Can't stop!"

After about three or four hours of this steady pace, the bait was gone, the deck full, and I was pooped out. But we were so pleased. It was only 30 nautical miles to our little port town of Morro Bay. And wow! We were headed home with a full load to finish the season!

Sometime later, in the middle of another albacore season, there was a big bite off Morro Bay in the same area where my honey and I first saw Irene. But now there was a tremendous fishing fleet out there. This included amateur fishermen who were new to the water and new to the profession. They were filling the radio air with their chatter, interfering with the passage of much needed information. There was one guy in particular, a real "Wanna Be." He was on the radio so much that it was hard for the "pros" to report to their running partners. Around mid-day, in-between the chatter, Irene tried to touch base with her partner. Each time she called in, the gabber jumped back on the air, preventing her from making contact. This went on for some time.

Then, when the "Wanna Be" finally stopped for a bit, Irene changed tactics and called him on the radio. The "Wanna Be" returned the call asking, "What do YOU want?"

Irene said, "I need to get through to my running partner. I need to see how he's doing. You need to let others have a turn."

This conversation was being broadcast across the entire fleet. Everyone was listening.

The guy answered, "Who are you anyway?! You're just a woman! This is a man's job. Go back to the kitchen where you belong!"

There was a moment of silence. Nothing. Then she came on the air. In a very low and clear voice she said, "My name is Irene." There was no further word from Irene for the rest of her trip.

About a week or so later those of us with a full catch headed in to Morro Bay to unload and get ready for another trip. But instead of going back out, the weather came up. More boats headed into port and those of us ready for the next trip had a chance to relax and visit with each other. I had my boat tied up on the second T dock, the one with the crane and the fish-buyer. I was with a small group of fishermen leaning against the rail, chatting and watching a larger group gathered on the dock halfway toward the beach. Most of the men in the larger group were inexperienced amateurs, and in the midst of them was that man, the "Wanna Be," with his back to the beach side.

Then I saw Irene. She piloted her boat over to the first T pier where the Coast Guard docked. She tied up and climbed from her vessel to the pier. She was looking fine, wearing a bright yellow dress with flowers down to just above her ankles. I pointed her out to my friends. "She's coming," I said and we watched as she came up the pier.

She walked right up to the "Wanna Be." He was of average height and build, but she was not. As she stood behind him, we could see how tall and strong she was. She tapped the the guy on the shoulder. He turned around and… Wham! She punched him right on the chin! He landed flat on his back. She stood over him with a fist on each hip.

"I've been fishing for a long time. When someone needs the radio, you shut up and listen. It's their turn. They might have something important to say. Information. Something that could help us all. Now, I'm Irene and don't you forget it!"

After that I added, "Tug Boat" to Irene's name. I didn't use it over the radio, of course, but just with the guys. When we were together talking about how Jo, or Pete, or Sam, were doing, it was "Tug Boat Irene" when we spoke about her.

What was left of the season was good. Later that winter I learned that Tug Boat Irene and her partner sold their two boats and got a larger one. She was the Captain and he was the Engineer. They were full partners in all that they did, in life as well as work. After a hand full of seasons more, they sold their boat and retired to their homeport of Eureka, California.

A handful of seasons again passed us by. The spring salmon season was transitioning to the albacore season for the summer. I was almost off the coast of Eureka and it was a good spot to make the change. When I got in and unloaded the salmon, I called Angela (my wife) to come up for a vacation while the changeover was going on. Driving up from Morro Bay she stopped off in Sausalito with a friend for the night. The next day, she made it up to Eureka by noon.

After we got everything done and ready, we took some time for fun and relaxation. And Irene came to mind. I said, "Tug Boat Irene and her partner live up here. Let's look them up!" We called and she invited us to her house for a visit. Angela had never met "Tug Boat Irene." She had only heard stories of a strong, independent woman who could stand her ground. When Irene opened the door, we were overwhelmed by her long, dark dress, her body like a model's, and her lovely face. Angela was shocked. Irene was in her 70's and beautiful! Her partner was in his 50s.

We had a really good time. As we were preparing to leave, I noticed one last surprise, a framed Doctorate degree on the wall by the door. Irene could have done anything. She chose to be a commercial fisherman.

Her name was Irene, and I never forgot it.

A FEW THOUGHTS AND EVENTS

Mid 2000s

Time is a device to create order for the undisciplined.

You can't go insane when your dignity is being washed
with a squirt to the face
from a squid,
hanging on a fish
hooked on my rockfish set line.

The contemporaries of a "creator" don't seem to believe it of him.
It takes the next generation to see the value,
but, as a rule, one way or another, it doesn't matter by then.

I pin my life
to a piece of geography
then hang my hopes on the wind.
When I sit back to look at them,
I find
they have moved.
I wonder—
Should I put them back in my pocket
or move my life over, too?

The moon in bloom
brings the tide in full,
then fades,
allowing the ebbing flow
to bring the land's tidings
of nourishment
to the hungry
awaiting in the depths.
I see in this
nature's rule
of all life
being on an endless ring.
If this be true,
oh God,

will I then have another turn?

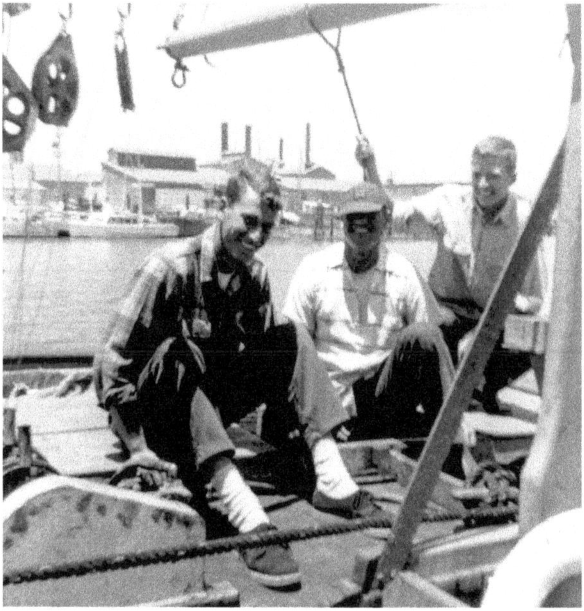

1964 Norman, Jim, and Dave, three fishing captains, in Sausalito off the Napa Street pier.

A FRIENDLY RACE WITH A FISHERMAN

Mid 1970s

Looking over the dark foreground of the sea
to the many-hued pink and glowing horizon of the East,
what do I see but the sparkling Golden Eye
rising brightly with a wink for me.

On its path, the Golden Eye from up on high, glowing.
daring me, in a sweat
to do the things I do best
before its daily duty ends.

Then, sliding down upon its red and yellow reflected pillar
to the West,
the Golden Eye slips between the waves to sleep.
Then, so must I.

THE EARLY ONE

Late 1960s

A bird
on the street
but by the wheel's will
already
its blood to lube.
its juices to cool.
its body to surface the road.
I thought hopefully
its spirit fluttered free.

A VIEW AT THE BEACH

1970

Hale, golden bodies,
health, youth and beauty
that build
pride and strength
from your position
of security.
Do leave some room
for a little compassion.

A CHILD GROWS

1977

The beautiful, absorbent child
descends
into the rough cocoon
of adolescence.
later
to emerge into
the wondrously varied world
of adulthood,
only having to choose
from among the verifications
for its own path
justification.

CIVILIZATION

Early 1970s

Civilization is a great, old, heavy, wooden, covered wagon
filled with all the people
standing on a road called "Progress."
There are no oxen at the yoke.
From about the middle of the wagon,
And back of each side, the road is weeds and dust.
Forward is grass and water
right in front of the yoke
covering the road.
From that point on is a thick fog
called "Knowledge and Achievement."

Once
In every age
an individual jumps out and pokes their head through the fog.
grabs the yoke, and breaks their ass
for a step or two
and then expires.
The line and fog move just that same distance forward.
Every few ages or so, after the individual has grabbed the yoke,
a handful of peers will jump down and take a quick peek.
Their help takes the wagon many additional steps onward and
when they expire
for a moment or two
the whole wagon has grass and water around it

FREE LOVE

In the day that this was written, all songs had been sung.
Free love, free love!

Everybody wants free love.

But, what do I do
with my emotions
after I've fallen in love
with you
and then
you're off
with someone else?

On that day everybody
wanted to play
but none knew how or wanted to pay.

Is this original?
I think not.

It only bespeaks of problems

that have been,
are now, and those to come.
While living in that day
with all the songs sung,
the blame for their problems was
on the fools and their ways
of the day before.
Oh!
What to do today
for survival
in the future?
It seems, as the song is sung,
diverting our attention laughingly
to them back there
we are still trying to move
toward that
Perfect Day

MANLY MARK

Sept. 1980

A man sat on a bench
with a moment to spare,
bare, sun burnt arms
resting on his knees,
thick curly hair
conspicuously glistening
in the late summer sun.

Certainly
a manly mark.

Eight years or so
the boy
arms clean, comely, round and shining
like a nectarine
who seemed struck
by the manly mark
attentively approached.

They bonded together in an understanding
at that moment
over just some hair.

The boy reached out and felt with his hand
once up, once down
on the mark
that one day would also be his.

Each
smiling contented
one, with what was
the other, with what would be
then on their separate way.

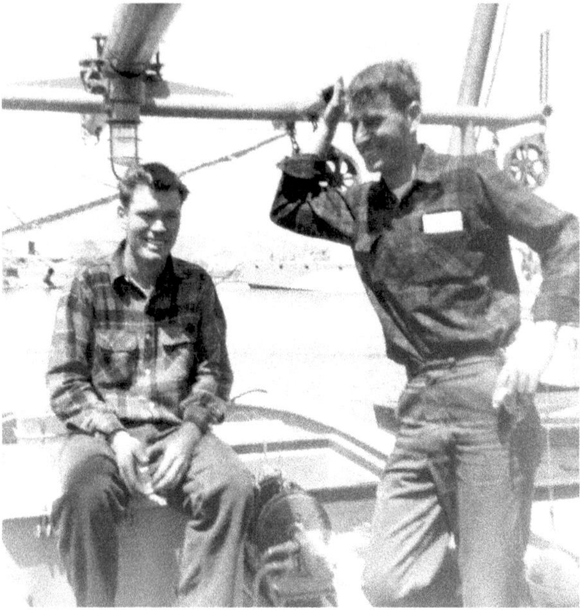

1964 Norman and Harlan in Sausalito off the Napa Street pier.

THE SEA

Late 1970s

Although of yourself
you are a still and placid thing,
you are also pliable.
By the will of other forces
and with strength beyond measure
you are moved and turned
to staggering shapes of power.

Yet, housed in you
is the substance of our existence.

With a small imagination
unequal to the task
we romanticize you into life.

So, armed with trust
in your sometime benevolence
and driven by our needs
we venture upon your surface.

Only to find a testing ground of our worth.

For the forces that drive you
also affect us
by pushing to their limits the fragile vessels in which we are carried
and stripping away our emotional and physical reserves.

We find that we cannot always survive your wrath.

WHAT IT TAKES FOR HUNTING A BIG CATCH

mid 1970s

All day
Dave and I wander
the hot, barren, glaring sea
looking to fill full our holds with fish.
Our lines
hanging limp
the holds are empty
crying, crying for fish

good fat fish.
Keep a' moving, Dave,
keep a' moving.
Don't turn back.
That was a teaser, Dave,
not a school of fish.
The sea is full of
scattered fish
so keep a' coming, Dave,
keep a' coming.

Although our holds are empty
and lines are hanging free
there is a circle ahead
awaiting there
with fish for you and me.
good, fat fish.
So keep a' coming, Dave,
don't turn back.
Up ahead and over the next swell
that hold-filling circle is there
awaiting for you and me.
The best is just ahead
awaiting for you and me.

A BIRTHDAY NIGHTMARE

Mid 1970s

First awareness
out of the hazy mist
upon a sparkling glassy sea
comes the little, shiny, new albacore vessel named Buck.

As Buck cruised smoothly out to the albacore grounds
he was instantly aware of his uniqueness
a supremely well-mounted
rudder and post
that gave him an edge for catching fish
and made him the envy of all the boats.

At the end of the season
all the female boats
would covetously admire his
rudder and post
and vie for the slip next his for the winter.

Year after year
Buck did so well that, on his birthdays
he would magnanimously try and tell the others
how he got his rudder and post the way it was,
so that they too could have more navigation control
and do better at fishing.

Things had been going so well for him for so long
that it was a shock to him, and everyone else,
when on one particular birthday
he was no longer the high liner.

All the boats shrank from him and whispered,
“He isn’t catching fish. What could be wrong?”
Then one said, “Do you suppose it could be
oh my!
the rudder post?”
Everybody gasped.

“Oh! He may become a hazard to navigation!”

“Hazard to navigation! Can’t have that!”
shouted the big, graveyard, steel-chomping tug.
“No! No!” Buck shouted “It’s just a little fish I can’t get”
taking firm grip on my rudder post.
“See! I’m not a hazard!”
The steel-chomping tug paid no attention
but came relentlessly onward.

“Can’t have a hazard to navigation!” and it took a chomp.
“Can’t have a hazard!” and it took another chomp.

“No! No!” screamed Buck. “It’s not my rudder post!
It’s the line-pullers, the line-pullers!”

“Can’t have a hazard!” the tug took another big chomp.
“Can’t have a hazard!” and the tug just kept on chomping.

Then Buck says “Oh! Ha! What the shit?
Wow! What a nightmare!”

Looking across his tummy and seeing what he had a grip of,
He asks, “What the hell is this?”

"Oh! Ha!" he exclaims.

Jumping up, Buck puts his boots on
and goes out to the rail,
looking around to check his position
as the night's accumulative pressure
is smoothly relieved.
He looks down and thinks with satisfaction
and a little relief,
"Hmm. Still well-mounted for a guy that's
done the rounds through 39!"

AN EXPERIENCE OF EXPRESSION

Out of your loss
will come fulfillment.

Although your words
may not truly express
what you mean
that is not necessary.

The sound of your voice
brings the meaning
from the depths of your heart
the good you wish upon us.

Out of your loss
will come your gain
for as one goes
another comes.

Although each is different
still
all is linked
by a fine thread.

Out of your loss
will come your victory
for out of your heart,
mind and soul,
the energy
will be sent on through
to ease another
as they ask for
the way to the path.

TROLLING AND DREAMS

Late 1960s

Trolling over the great depths
with lures and bared hooks trailing free.

Hoping to make the big catch.

Like in my dreams
to catch
the beautiful mermaid
I swim with my lure
My penis hanging free.

All I get for my troubles
are rusty hooks
from traveling
in barren waters.

As in the dream
all I get
is a swollen end on my prick
from scraping
the sandy bottom.

CHASING THE BONANZA

I sailed all day and slept all night
when I got to where I was suppose to be

I slept all day and rolled all night

then I asked
where is it
the place I'm looking for

Someone then said
ya big dummy
back where you came from

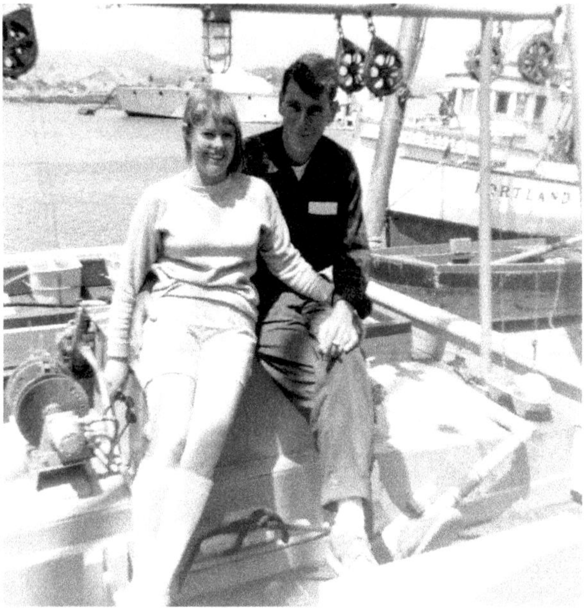

1964 Norman and Angela off Napa Street pier in Sausalito.

MIGHT IS RIGHT

How much right
does might have?
Just because
right has some might
if might has the last word
for now
what does
right
have the last of

Year older

Another year older
another day in debt
no wiser for the mileage
but still happy
to have been born
this day
long, long ago.

Now that I am an old timer
I think I'm that smarter
doing what I think I have ta'
—out here
where I oughtn't
just to get back
to where I started.

LLOYD BOY

When I hear you
I think of that
old man river
who's seen so much
sorrow and pain
but keeps running on
when a lesser spirit
would cease to go.

The river
slows its pace
at the drag of the deep.
So it may seem
to you
your efforts
go for naught.

But the river does
reach its home
the sea.

Its lion's heart and
spirit to go on
should encourage you.

MY KINGDOM FOR A HORSE

You know the story.
Well of course
I would not presume
to compare my boat
to a kingdom
or my problem
of no fish
to that of the noble kings.

And would I trade my boat?
Hell no!
But if I could
Just catch a few
'd trade
my energy
hard labor and sweat
for them.

THOUGHTS OF THIS & THAT

6-12-1977 Mid or late 70s

If
the eye for an eye
hand for a hand
life for a life
is biblical and historical justice
for a man

and since nations
are made of
more than one
with consent as extensions
of themselves
it would then stand
for nations to pay
the same way
as the bodies that make them up.

According to history's records

if all accounts
were called due and payable
every nation would be totally bankrupt.
Oh well
that would end
the over-population problem.

The contemporaries of a creator
don't seem to believe it of him.
It takes the next
generation to see the value.
But as a rule
one way or another
it doesn't matter by then.

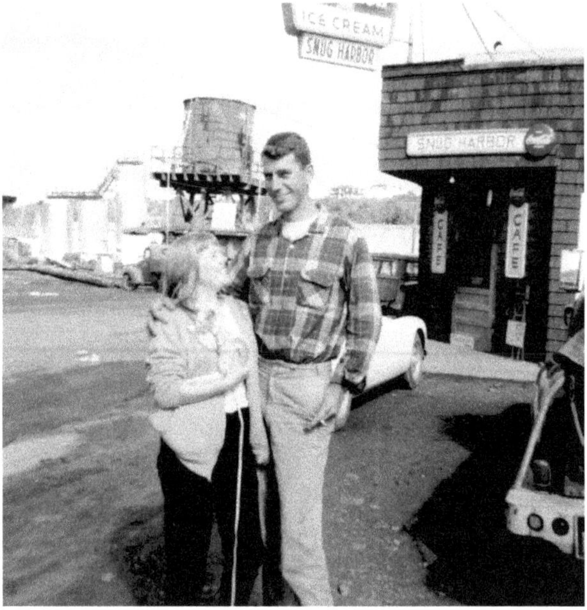

1963 Norman and Angela. Snug Harbor Cafe in Oakland.

VALUE OF A LIFE

I have contemplated

the value of a life
by the stimulation of my
emotions at various times

From odd experiences
of losing loved ones
seeing others
reacting to the same
or in lonely moments
deluding myself
that I have the answer

Or know what I would do
after reading a romanticized other's view
cluck-clucking and "Oh-my-God" -ing!
over a devastating disaster each view changing
in intensity
with my age and strength.

One might come
to the conclusion
that a life about to be lost
would have an answer.

The moment
I think
that one
is about to lose or
take a life
the value may be known.

YOUNG WOMAN IN ARMOR

Mid 1970s

Inside a slightly grotesque
suit of armor
made of flesh
with an outline of femininity
that had one shapeless
fleshier leg
larger than the other
with a few hard knots
which considering
that other
was not without a pleasing shape.
The body was not overly large
but was protruding
a round tummy
with pronounced hips and
two meaty chunks for a fanny
all tapering up to narrow shoulders
with a straight back and a short
thick neck.

The arms were
of normal length
each section round, meaty, and firm.

The hands and fingers were short and square.

Stuck on top of all this
was a round head
with a striking face of freckles
and full lips
a short turned-up nose
and straight, brown hair
that was very fine.

All was clean.

Large, clear, round brown eyes that glowed and sparkled
if paid attention to
revealed a beautiful, clever, mischievous child
that could make the shielding body move
with a subtle grace.

BEGIN TO END

In my youth
my head was empty
but I had health
stamina and resilient muscles
Forever seemed to be in front of me
no care had I.

As I grew older
my muscles slackened and stamina shortened.
The realization of my mortality
filled my head.
With this bit of wisdom
I turned to see the next in line
only to see myself as a youth.

Turning again

to proceed on to my time
I wondered
who might have benefited
from my passing by.

NO PAIN KNOW I

No pain know I
but my own
although
by suffering enough
of others' sorrows
I then know.

No pain know I
but my own
although
by suffering enough
of others' sorrows
I have then seen all.

SOUL MATE

Mid 1970s

No other communication can beat that of two
in the relationships
of human kind.
For out of that number
comes another
to renew and replenish
not only the race
but the enthusiasm and zest
for living.
And after their fruit
has grown and gone
they can walk
through the corridor of life
with ease and understanding
that no casual
connection can attain.

ALONE, BUT NOT

Oh the night is dark

the sea is deep
and I am alone
on my boat.
But I see around me
the lights of the fleet
like stars so far
and yet
their glow seems so near.
With radio to bridge the space
I know
that I'm not alone.

A FISHERMAN'S MONOLOGUE: THE HERO

To fish or not to fish
that is
a good question
why is it
to have made this choice
for a living
I have to suffer
the wave and spray

Is it truly noble
to be a hero
to kill 500 fish a day
if only I could

Well one day I did
and that same day
somebody got a 1000

Oh well
the pain of it all

I travel far and wide
over calm and stormy seas
to kill a fish
and suffering
in the icy hell
of the hold

Time paces
In the middle of a trip comes
the storm
of the year
and I run for my life
because really I'm tired

but I say
my pump is out
to save face
but then I find
Joe stayed out with a smaller boat
oh shit
my reputation's ruined

Soon we're out
snorting and growling
at the next hot spot
hey, don't you cut my circle you damn fool
I'll cut your lines

Ah
one fine day
the sea is calm
the sky is clear
but no fish
and who do I see over there
Pete
the hottest fisherman
out of that near port
he knows where he's going
I'll just follow him
For hours
and no fish

Hey Pete, I call,
where're we going
I don't know, he says
I was following you
Oh God, we're in trouble

The finer moments
always seem to come to mind
trips of 30 days
and endurance to defy Hercules
oh my aching back
with memories of long
dark, rolling, pitching, sleepless nights
Ah that question
the answer
it's becoming more obvious
I don't have to take this

but then the season does end
and at last I'm home
and I find the bills have been paid
and my wife
she says
my hero, you are back
and of course
to that I say
Honey for you
I'll go fishing anytime.

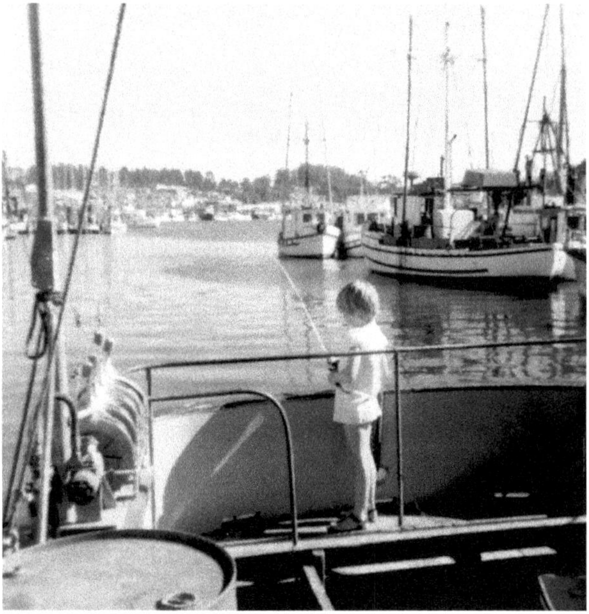

1971 Robbin fishing off the back of her father's boat in Morro Bay.

CHALLENGE AND RELATIONSHIP

Early 1970s

Standing at the stern
with hair blown wild
from wind and no care
and the rigging whistling
a fearful warning

waiting for duty's call
of fish
to fill the pitching boat's hold

teeth flashing
from the good feeling within
that the ocean's challenge
can be met

with the storm's help
the seas' passions aroused
and the stern mistress
like a lover
sends a salty cold kiss
before the battle begins

TWO POEMS FOR MY DOG

1975 mid 1970s

As I sit
in my lordly position
catching the story-telling smells on the breeze
and eyeing to the limit
the horizons of my world

I contemplate
the right of my freedom
given by the strength of leg
that gives ease to my mobility

I imagine
as I move
my mastery of all I survey
and, as I survey
I am master of all I see

Oh, a call

Ah it is time
MY master

with a biscuit for me

MEDITATIONS ON THE COLLIE

Man's imagination
makes him great
but in spite of this
at the same time
he's afraid
of the different and the unknown

in order to protect himself
he will delegate the responsibility
for himself to a law
consequently tying himself down

Some of mankind's forward-stepping achievements
and most of his foreword-stepping knowledge
even to what freedoms are available
come from individuals who took the consequences for their actions
and didn't turn back for the security
of a master's biscuit

A THOUGHT ON CYRANO DE BERGERAC

I have written a verse or two
but tonight
my inspiration comes from
Cyrano de Bergerac
and my minute glory of verse
must bow before a master
as I grasp
my fleeting thoughts
racing through the corridors
of my undisciplined brain
like the shadows
before the swift brightening dawn
my memory strains to hold
a meaningful coherent word

what matters who wrote what
blessed are the minds
that hold
the inspiration
to lift humanity

FRIENDSHIP

1978

Friendship is an immeasurable commodity
of energy
that can't be asked for
bought or taken

It needs no particular reason
but can only be given
in one direction
depending on the supply
for a specific duration

To maintain
a continued flow
the supply
must be replaced
exactly as received
—freely

AWAKENING

Toot your horn
throw a can
are the suggestions
but to no avail

he is not brought
from sleep

Soon though
in his way
he comes awake

looking about
he sees his fellows
dispersing
from the morning bite

after checking the scores
he's heard to say
well good ole me
I've awakened
at the hot spot again

A FEW THOUGHTS AND EVENTS

Mid 2000s

Time is a device to create order for the undisciplined

You can't go insane when your dignity is being washed
with a squirt in the face
from a squid
hanging on a fish
hooked on my rockfish set line

The contemporaries of a creator don't seem to believe it of him
it takes the next generation to see the value
but as a rule
one way or another
it doesn't matter by then

I pin my life
to a piece of geography
then hang my hopes on the wind

When I sit back to view them
I find
they have moved
I wonder
should I put them back
in my pocket
or move my life over too?

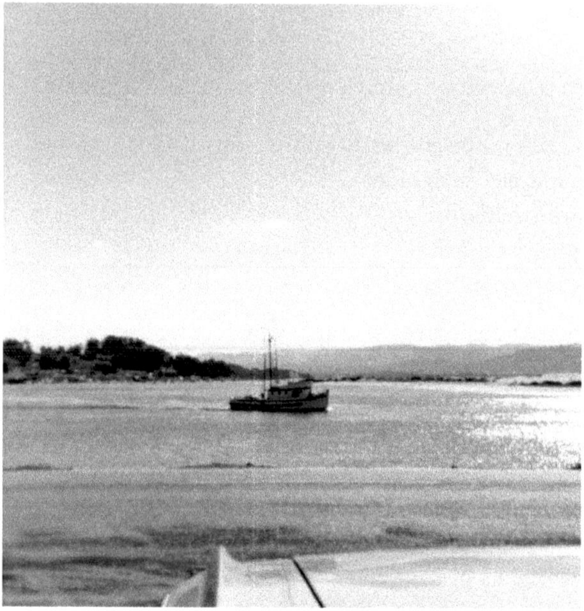

1971 *The Mangoe* heading out from Morro Bay.

THE MOON IN BLOOM

Mid 2000s

The moon in bloom
brings the tide in full
then fades
allowing the ebbing flow
to bring the land's tidings
of nourishment
to the hungry
awaiting in the depths

I see in this
nature's rule
of all life
being on an endless ring

If this be true
Oh God
will I then have another turn?

WARS

In any battle
glory is drowned in gore
heroics are dulled
by repetitive acts for survival
exhaustion and indecision
are the order of the day

SHORT LIVES

Life
like a meteor
is a short-lived glow

It seems a shame
that unlike the meteorite
more don't get through
to make a significant impact
on our world

DAVIE

There is a Davie
not Davie the Crockett
but Davie of the fleet's own
troubadour of the seas
on his boat
with his family around him
Cindy and big Baboo
the 2-foot giant

His heart is full
so he has to sing
that we may share
in his joy

BOWL

Noel the bowl
can hold all
spooning out just enough
with a song to please
or a word to rein in those that run
without a thought
Noel the bowl
has enough for all

INNER ENERGY

As measured time turns
at the mark
I grow older

The saying is
"oh, my lost youth"
but I say
I have left
nothing behind

For with each new experience
whatever it may be
my horizons are added to
my mind is growing
my awareness
expanding

I have left
nothing behind

As my body grows tired and withers
I do not fear

For like the stars in the universe
that exhaust their fire
then implode
into the hole again
like the momentary pain
of birth
death is the door
for new splendor

For as stars die
their dust
reused and renewed
so is man's energy
reused and renewed
for new and better things

So I have left
nothing behind

FREEDOM AT A COST

1970s

How much freedom
must I sacrifice
in an endeavor
to maintain an authority
that dictates to the might
supposedly placed
to *preserve*
my freedom?

A NEW TOOL

3-2-2012 early 2000s

No more
will I just drift through life

Not with the new tool
I've acquired

That brought meaning and depth
to my existence

My soul mate.

JOHN AND HIS "SANAK"

There is a girl that I love
and she loves me
we plan to get married
next year in June

But I'm a fisherman
to my profession I have long been true
and have to catch so much fish
to make do
for my true love and I

But as luck would have it
the engine brakes down
and the radio needs replacing
So my lady love and I
will live and wait
'til the next year in June

But you know
if you be a fisherman
that which happens
is beyond control

A season of poor fishing passes us by
So my love and I will slide along too
As next year in June
for one reason or another
and much ribbing from my friends
comes and goes

My love and I know it's all right
she's for me and I'm for her

Well as fate would have it
the time has arrived as all old fishermen know
I can't untie the lines from the dock anymore
So I tell my true love
It's time and I'm ready

My true love says to me
here now there is no need
the children are grown and gone
and I have social security and women's lib
my vibrator too
So back to the deep blue sea with you

TOM'S LAMENT:TO BE THE HIGH LINER

Why oh why
does it seem
as I pass by
others are pulling in
more fish than I

It has to be
this boat is in trouble
that's why
they're beating me

But I have balance lights
That tells me everything's
as it should be

Oh! Oh!
What can
the matter be?

At the day's end
the tallies are in
Tom has actually left
the fleet far behind

So we all know
wherein
his troubles lay
it's between his ears!

LOVE

2003

Written for Robbin & Kevin's Wedding

Like a river
Flows in one direction
Its source is great
Its course and intent
Unconditional

But even so
Can be exhausted
Unless replenished as received
In the same manner
Unconditionally

The river's purpose
Is to feed the sea
The sea's purpose
Is to return the source
By rain clouds
That is
The river's reservoir

Two means of expression
In forms of energy and manner
So different
But still able to create
A cycle of life

MY BOAT MY BOAT

1970s

How can I
truly
describe my feelings
about what
in reality
is only a tractor of the sea,
plowing a furrow
back and forth
all day
to get fish.
As many as I can, of course.

Unlike on the farm
I can't get off,
can't go up to the house
to see my wife,
have lunch or a snack—
because I'm out to sea
twenty-five days or longer
throughout most of the year.

With the end of each trip
I unload,
Cleanup,
square away and supply,
kiss the wife and kids,
then sail away again
out to sea.

In my spare time
in the off-season
I worry and work
over this thing
like no other man works,
for not only is this tool my livelihood,
it is the holder
and carrier
of my life.

Like my wife,
My boat is a carrier
of my heart
through troubled and hard times.

On its back is the cabin
like a trailer.
There I live and work.
By stepping out the door
I'm on the job.
Stepping in,
I'm out of the weather
Sometimes I get up and look out
to calm seas and warm weather and
I'm happy and I say,
Well ole gal
what a day,
let's get 'em.

The boat is made of wood,
nails and bolts,
like skin and bone
and not unlike the fingers of the hands
laced together
to the right shape.

Sometimes through a long night
drifting
on a moderately rough sea.
the boat is rolling and
sorta heavy.
Laying in my bunk
I hear the planks
creaking and groaning
kinda like my old knees.

If there is a terrible storm and it takes a big heave
in a moment of fear
I might say,
Oh gal
hang together,
don't let me drown.

As usual, it survives
for it was made well.

Yes, I like my boat,
Though sometimes when I'm tired,
I can't stand it.
Yet, out of all it could have been made,
Steel,
Plastic,
Fiberglass,
I like its material the best.

You might say
that my feelings for it
are love,
and I can imagine that this vessel has an awareness
of the fragile being it carries.

After all,
it was made
from a living thing.

THE LEGEND OF WEASEL SLEEPING THROUGH THE MORNING CATCH

Mid 1970s

On one particularly calm and balmy day in the late seasonal fishery, when the pressure was off and the fish were down in the cooler depths and off the bite, a fellow fisherman in his boat and in a mood not to let the day slip slowly by, asks Weasel if he is of a similar mind for a barbeque and a shot of wine aboard his boat. "Ah yes," is Weasel's reply.

So, the tall tales with wine flow till early morn'. Then,
getting to his friendly bunk for a wink before the dawn,
Weasel must have been a chuckling, hassle of a sight.

Of course, by now you've guessed,
Awakening him is at best a test,
and furthermore, don't 'cha know,
this is the morning, the fish choose to show.

So, all his friends, in the same game,
pulling in the fish as they came,
and using Weasel's vessel as the marker for the school,
laugh, as they worry and fret on how to wake the dreaming fool.

Purchase and Download ebook

https://www.kobo.com/us/en/ebook/down-to-sea-in-little-boats

Lightning Source UK Ltd.
Milton Keynes UK
UKHW022145090223
416682UK00016B/2292